Read & Respond

FOR KS2

Bill's New Frock
Teachers' notes 3

Guided reading
Teachers' notes 4

Shared reading
Teachers' notes 7
Photocopiable extracts 8

Plot, character and setting
Activity notes 11
Photocopiable activities 15

Talk about it
Activity notes 19
Photocopiable activities 22

Get writing
Activity notes 25
Photocopiable activities 28

Assessment
Teachers' notes and activity 31
Photocopiable activity 32

Read & Respond

FOR KS2

Author: Gillian Howell

Development Editor: Simret Brar

Editor: Marion Archer

Assistant Editor: Alex Albrighton

Series Designer: Anna Oliwa

Designer: Liz Gilbert

Illustrations: Philippe Dupasquier

Text © Gillian Howell © 2009 Scholastic Ltd

Designed using Adobe InDesign

Published by Scholastic Ltd, Villiers House,
Clarendon Avenue, Leamington Spa,
Warwickshire CV32 5PR

www.scholastic.co.uk

Printed by Bell & Bain

1 2 3 4 5 6 7 8 9   9 0 1 2 3 4 5 6 7 8

British Library Cataloguing-in-Publication Data
A catalogue record for this book is available from the British Library.

ISBN 978-1407-11242-8

The rights of Gillian Howell to be recognised as the author of this work have been asserted by her in accordance with the Copyright, Designs and Patents Act 1988.

Extracts from the Primary National Strategy's *Primary Framework for Literacy* (2006) www.standards.dfes.gov.uk/primaryframework © Crown copyright. Reproduced under the terms of the Click Use Licence.

All rights reserved. This book is sold subject to the condition that it shall not, by way of trade or otherwise, be lent, hired out or otherwise circulated without the publisher's prior consent in any form of binding or cover other than that in which it is published and without a similar condition, including this condition, being imposed upon the subsequent purchaser.

No part of this publication may be reproduced, stored in a retrieval system, or transmitted, in any form or by any means, electronic, mechanical, photocopying, recording or otherwise, without the prior permission of the publisher. This book remains copyright, although permission is granted to copy pages where indicated for classroom distribution and use only in the school which has purchased the book, or by the teacher who has purchased the book, and in accordance with the CLA licensing agreement. Photocopying permission is given only for purchasers and not for borrowers of books from any lending service.

Acknowledgements

The publishers would like to thank **Egmont UK** for the use of text extracts and illustrations from *Bill's New Frock* by Anne Fine. Text © 1989, Anne Fine (1989, Egmont); Illustrations © 1989 Philippe Dupasquier. Every effort has been made to trace copyright holders for the works reproduced in this book, and the publishers apologise for any inadvertent omissions.

Bill's New Frock

SECTION 1

About the book

Bill's New Frock was written in 1989 by Anne Fine and revised in 2002. The hero of the story, Bill Simpson, wakes one morning and finds he has suddenly and inexplicably become a girl. The story is written with a lot of humour and vivid description about Bill's predicament, embarrassment and horror in seven chapters. It raises the issue of how girls are sometimes treated differently to boys, and what is fair and unfair about people's assumptions about boys' and girls' behaviour and abilities.

Plot summary

In the opening chapter, the light-hearted tone of the story is established by Bill's parents' lack of reaction to the discovery. They don't notice anything strange, in fact, his mother insists he wears a pink frock to school and his father calls him 'poppet' and tells him he looks sweet.

On the way to school, Mean Malcolm whistles at him instead of kicking him, which Bill finds even worse. During the day, Bill is expected to be neat and gets into trouble for messy handwriting. In the playground, he discovers boys dominate it with their football game, leaving no room for the girls.

As the day progresses, Bill finds dresses impractical as his begins to get very dirty. When Bill is left with only girls' comics to read during a wet lunchtime he gets angry and fights a boy. However, at this point Bill realises that there is an advantage to wearing a frock when the boy is blamed for the fight.

After break, the rain stops so the class go outside for races. Three girls hatch a plan to let Paul, who is disabled, win the final race. Bill is included in the plan but finds he wants to win.

The girls are furious with Bill, but Paul is so thrilled at coming second they forgive Bill.

Both Kirsty and Mrs Collins tell Bill he doesn't look quite right today. Then, on the way home Bill sees Mean Malcolm who whistles at him again. Bill stands up for himself and teaches Malcolm a lesson about respect.

At home, his mother is horrified by the state of his dress, sending him to get changed and declaring never again to send him to school in a dress. Bill gets changed, looks in the mirror and is relieved and delighted to discover he is a boy again.

About the author

Anne Fine was born in the Midlands and studied history and politics at university. She had various jobs before writing her first book in 1971, when her eldest daughter was a baby. She has written over 25 books for all ages, from young readers to adults. She mostly writes humorous books and, particularly for younger readers, books that raise fairly serious social issues.

Anne was the Children's Laureate between 2001 and 2003. She was awarded an OBE in the Queen's Birthday Honours List in 2003 for Services to Literature.

Facts and figures
Bill's New Frock won the Smarties Prize in 1989. Other award-winning books by Anne Fine include: *Flour Babies,* winner of both the Whitbread Children's Book of the Year Award and the Carnegie Medal; and *Goggle-Eyes*, which as well as winning the Carnegie Medal and the Guardian Children's Fiction Award, was adapted for BBC television.
Madame Doubtfire has also been made into a film.

Guided reading

SECTION 2

Introducing the book

Show the front cover to the children and read the title of the book. Ask the children if any of them already know this story and who wrote it. Invite them to find and read the name of the author. Ask the children if they have read any other books written by Anne Fine. Discuss the type of stories they are and encourage them to compare any similarities or differences in the style and themes of the stories. If any of the children have already read the book, explain that reading it again in a group will help them explore the story in greater detail, but tell them not to spoil the plot for other readers.

Turn to the back cover and read the blurb. Ask them to suggest what sort of things Bill discovers are different for girls. Invite them to say what sort of story they expect this to be. Do they think it will be exciting, frightening, serious or funny? Encourage the children to give reasons for their opinions based on their knowledge of other Anne Fine books or on the wording of the title.

A really awful start

Identify any vocabulary that might be challenging before the children begin to read – for example, 'haphazardly' on page 13. Remind the children to use their knowledge of phonics and syllables to segment and blend any words they are unsure about. Read the opening sentence to the group. Encourage the children to say what they would think and feel if this happened to them. Ask them if they think this is an effective way to begin the story. Does it make them want to find out why and how Bill has become a girl, or do they think it might be a joke?

Tell them to read to the end of the chapter and then describe what happens to Bill. Ask them to say how Bill reacts to being dressed in a frock and find the words in the text ('"This can't be true," Bill Simpson said to himself.' on page 3). Invite the children to find three things that make Bill feel embarrassed and three things that make him feel resentful or angry about how he is treated, and ask them to show you the evidence in the text. Encourage the children to say what sort of person they think Bill is.

Discuss the tone of the story with the children. Do they think it is a realistic, serious story or light-hearted and humorous? Encourage them to support their opinion with evidence from the text – for example, it is humorous because no one thinks it is strange that Bill is a girl.

Invite the children to find and read the last sentence in the chapter. Do they think this is a good way to end a chapter? Does it make them want to find out what happens next? Ask them to predict what Bill might do at playtime.

The wumpy choo

Turn to page 27 and ask the children to look at the illustration. Invite them to say what they think is happening. You might like to take a few minutes to talk about games they play at break times and whether the boys and girls play together or separately and why.

Invite the class to read to the end of the chapter and then explain why Bill doesn't join in with the boys' football game. Ask them if they think the boys would have allowed Bill to play had he tried to join in and to give a reason for their opinion. Invite them to explain the bet and why Bill decides to take the bet. Ask: *How do the boys react at first? What does Bill think is different about their reaction and why? What do the boys tell Bill to do? Does Bill think the boys are fair or unfair to the girls in the playground?* Encourage the children to show you the evidence for their answers in the text. Ask the class to turn back to page 21 and to tell you if they knew what a 'wumpy choo' was. Were they surprised to find out what it was? Do they think Bill is disappointed to find out it is a 1p chew? Ensure they support their reasons using evidence from the text.

Guided reading

Pink, pink, nothing but pink

Tell the children to read the chapter. When they have finished, encourage them to describe Bill's reaction to being chosen as a model and find the evidence in the text. ('"No!" Bill said. "No, no, no! Not me! Absolutely not! You can't!"' on page 34.) In this chapter, the author uses two ways to show emphasis. Invite the children to find examples of where the author has used exclamation marks and italics for emphasis. Ask the children to find the sentences where italics are used and to read them aloud with expressive voices.

Encourage the children to explain why Bill eventually gives up his resistance. What do they think they would have done in Bill's situation? Ask them to read the first paragraph on page 40, beginning 'Bill ignored everyone'. Invite the class to suggest what Bill might have been thinking to himself as he just sat there being painted.

No pockets

Before beginning to read, find the secretary's name, Mrs Bandaraina, on page 42. If anyone has difficulty in reading the name, encourage them to break it into syllables, 'Ban/da/rain/a' and then blend it quickly together. Invite the children to read the opening paragraph on page 41. Ask them if Bill thinks being chosen to take the key to the office is a good or bad thing and why. Do the children in the group enjoy being chosen for errands? Invite them to explain why they like or dislike it. Ask them to look at the chapter title 'No pockets' and predict what might happen in the chapter. Explain that Bill suffers a dilemma at the beginning of the chapter. Tell the children to read to the end of the first paragraph on page 44 and then to explain Bill's dilemma. Do they think this adds to the humour of the story?

Invite the children to read to the end of the chapter and then describe the other things Bill takes to the office. Can the children explain how the author builds an air of tension as each item is added to Bill's errand? For example, the ink is in glass bottles and he is warned not to drop them, the medical forms are in perfect alphabetical order and the warning is repeated. Ask: *What causes Bill to drop everything and what is the result? How does Bill feel about his frock now?*

The big fight

Invite the children to read to the end of page 63. Ask them to predict what they think Bill will do. Do the children think Bill will swap the *Dandy* for another girls' comic (*June*), given that he has actually enjoyed reading *Bunty*? Encourage them to give a reason for their opinion.

Tell the class to read to the end of the chapter, describe what happens and explain how the author builds up the atmosphere leading to the big fight. Encourage each child to find an example of where italics are used for emphasis and to read them using expressive voices. Turn to page 68 and point out Mrs Collins' words when she stops the fight. Ask: *Why does the author write 'dare' in italics and in upper case?* Invite them to read her words with appropriate expression. Turn to page 70 and ask the children to explain the different use of italics for *'Fighting is stupid and fighting is ugly'*. Encourage the children to suggest why the other pupils in Bill's class whisper different things to Rohan and to Bill. Do they think they both deserve their punishment by Mrs Collins or the sympathy from the others?

Letting Paul win

Invite the children to read to the end of the chapter and then describe what happens. Turn to page 72 and ask why Mrs Collins shakes her head 'in quiet disbelief'. What do they think Mrs Collins is thinking? Ask the children why Mrs Collins decides to take the class outside and what effect it has on the children.

Tell them to re-read the passage when the

Guided reading

SECTION 2

girls plan to let Paul win the final race on pages 77–80. Ask: *Why do the girls make the plan? How does Bill react to it?* Encourage them to explain what reasons Bill gives himself for letting Paul win and why he then does not follow the plan. Invite them to explain why Bill's winning is the better outcome to the race. Discuss with the children why they think Kirsty suddenly remarks that Bill is different today and how Bill reacts to this comment. Ask them to summarise how Bill is feeling at the end of this chapter.

Happy ending

Read the chapter heading and encourage the children to predict what the happy ending will be. Tell them to read to the end of the book and describe what happens in this chapter. Invite them to explain why they think Bill reacts as he does to Mean Malcolm's whistle. Do they think it was right and why? Encourage the children to skim-read the opening chapter again and find events and characters that also feature in the final chapter. (For example, Bella the cat doesn't notice any difference, Mean Malcolm whistles at Bill and Mrs Collins comments that Bill is not quite right.) Tell them to check the order of these events. (They are in reverse order in the last chapter.) Ask the children if they think this is an effective way to finish a story and encourage them to explain why it works well. Can they think of any other stories that use this device to finish?

Discuss the story as a whole. Invite them to say what they think the story is about and what the main theme is. Take a few minutes to discuss how girls and boys are treated. Do they think girls and boys are expected to behave differently? Do they think this is fair?

Shared reading

SECTION 3

Extract 1

- Recap how Bill has been sent to school in a pink frock and everyone is treating him as if he is a girl.
- Encourage the children to read aloud with you. Invite them to identify the spoken words and to point out the speech punctuation. Highlight the words 'chewed' and 'me' and ask them why these words have been written in italics. Tell them to scan the text to find other examples of italics used for emphasis.
- Read the first sentence together and invite the children to suggest why Bill puts his head in his hands. What do they imagine Bill is thinking?
- Continue reading up to the end of the paragraph ending 'as in a dream'. Ask the children to explain why they think Bill can't help just getting on with his work and what else he could have done. What sort of reaction do they think Bill would have got if he had pointed out that he was a boy wearing a dress?
- Read to the end of the extract. Ask: *How does the author show the unfairness of the situation?* Discuss whether it is true that all girls are always neater than all boys.

Extract 2

- This extract is from Chapter 3, when Mrs Collins can only find pink paint and so Bill is chosen to be the class model because his dress is pink.
- The extract includes dialogue between Bill and Mrs Collins. Point out how a change of speaker begins on a new line. Ask volunteers to highlight the punctuation used in writing dialogue.
- Read together from the beginning up to and including '"Perfect!" said Mrs Collins'. Choose two children to be Mrs Collins and Bill, or divide the class into two groups. Together, read only the spoken words using expressive voices. Encourage the children to read the words in italic print with emphasis.
- Read to the end of the extract and ask the children to suggest what Bill might do next. Would he continue to resist Mrs Collins or would he give in? Ask them to give reasons for their ideas and to say what they would do in Bill's situation.
- Remind the children about the conventions for using adverbs. Together, go through the text and highlight the adverbs to revise their use and spelling. (They include *closely, slowly, beautifully, firmly, clearly* and *suddenly*.)

Extract 3

- Explain that this extract comes from the final chapter of the story, as Bill is going home.
- Read together up to the words 'he took it so very badly'. Discuss the state of the pink frock. Ask: *Is it only the state of the dress that makes Bill react badly to the whistle? Is it all the things that have gone wrong during the day? Is it because Mean Malcolm thinks Bill is a girl?* Encourage the children to expand their suggestions by giving reasons for their ideas. Discuss what they might do if someone whistled at them.
- Read to the end of the extract. Invite volunteers to take turns to read Bill's spoken words with expressive voices. Encourage the children to explain what is in the text that helps them to read with expression (italics and punctuation).
- Ask the class to think about how Bill would feel after he pushes Mean Malcolm off the dustbin. Can they suggest how Mean Malcolm would react to being pushed? Gather the children's thoughts then read the rest the next few paragraphs from the book to the children. Were they right?

READ & RESPOND: Activities based on Bill's New Frock

Shared reading

SECTION 3

Extract 1

A really awful start

Bill Simpson put his head in his hands and covered his eyes.

'On with your work down there on table five,' warned Mrs Collins promptly.

She meant him. He knew it. So Bill picked up his pen and opened his books. He couldn't help it. He didn't seem to have any choice. Things were still going on in their own way, as in a dream.

He wrote more than he usually did. He wrote it more neatly than usual, too. If you looked back through the last few pages of his work book, you'd see he'd done a really good job, for him.

But you wouldn't have thought so, the way Mrs Collins went on when she saw it.

'Look at this,' she scolded, stabbing her finger down on the page. 'This isn't very neat, is it? Look at this dirty smudge. And the edge of your book looks as if it's been *chewed!*'

She turned to Philip to inspect his book next. It was far messier than Bill's. It was more smudgy and more chewed-looking. The writing was untidy and irregular. Some of the letters were so enormous they looked like giants herding the smaller letters haphazardly across the page.

'Not bad at all, Philip,' she said. 'Keep up the good work.'

Bill could scarcely believe his ears. He was outraged. As soon as she'd moved off, he reached out for Philip's book, laid it beside his own on the table, and compared the two.

'It isn't fair!' he complained bitterly. 'Your page is *much* worse than my page. She didn't say anything nice to *me.*'

Philip just shrugged and said:

'Well, girls are neater.'

Text © 1989, Anne Fine.

PHOTOCOPIABLE

READ & RESPOND: Activities based on *Bill's New Frock*

Shared reading

Extract 2

Pink, pink, nothing but pink

'No!' Bill said. 'No, no, no! Not me! Absolutely not! You can't!'

Now everyone turned to look at Bill.

'No!' Bill insisted. 'I am *not all pink*!'

Now Mrs Collins, too, was inspecting Bill closely.

'Pink frock,' she admitted slowly. 'And fiery hair. Rich rosy freckles and a nice deep blush. Yes, you'll do beautifully, dear. You're all pink.'

'I am *not pink*.'

But he was getting pinker by the minute. And by the time everyone had wandered back to their seats clutching their little plastic tubs of paint, you wouldn't have needed any other colour to do a really fine portrait of him.

'Perfect!' said Mrs Collins.

And taking Bill Simpson firmly by the hand, she tried to lead him over towards a chair in the middle of the room, where everyone would be able to see him clearly while they were painting him.

Bill tried to pull back. Mrs Collins turned in astonishment at his unwillingness, and let go of his hand quite suddenly. Bill staggered back – straight into Nicky who had just prised the top off his paint tub.

A huge glob of pink paint flew up in the air and landed on Bill Simpson's frock. As everyone watched, it gathered itself, all fat and heavy at the bottom. Then, slowly, it slithered down between the folds of material, leaving a thick pink slug trail.

Bill Simpson watched in silence as a small pool of pink paint appeared on the floor, beside his left foot.

Text © 1989, Anne Fine.

Shared reading

SECTION 3

Extract 3

Happy ending

Mean Malcolm saw him coming, and whistled.

Bill looked a sight. He knew it. The frock was a rumpled mess, with grubby fingerprints all round the hem, a huge, brown football-shaped smudge on the front, paint smears down the folds, rips in each side where he had hunted in vain for pockets, a great criss-cross footprint where Rohan kicked him, and grass stains down the back – the sort of grass stains that *never* come out.

The frock was a disaster.

And that is probably why, when Mean Malcolm whistled at Bill Simpson again, he took it so very badly.

He stopped and glowered at Mean Malcolm.

'Whistling at *me*?'

Mean Malcolm looked astonished to find this pink apparition glaring at him with such menace. He shifted uneasily on the lid of his dustbin.

'*Because*,' continued Bill savagely, 'I am not a *dog*! I am –' He hesitated a moment, not knowing quite how to finish, then yelled triumphantly:

'I am a *person*!'

And charging at Mean Malcolm with all the pent-up fury of the most horrible and frustrating day in his life, he flung him backwards off the dustbin lid, into a pile of spilled rubbish.

'There!' he yelled. 'That will teach you! Whistle at dogs in future – not at people!'

Text © 1989, Anne Fine.

Plot, character and setting

SECTION 4

It isn't fair!

Objective: To empathise with characters.
What you need: Copies of *Bill's New Frock*, photocopiable page 15, scissors.
Cross-curricular links: PSHE; Citizenship.

What to do
- Use this activity after reading Chapters 1 and 2. Discuss with the children how they feel when they think they have been treated unfairly. Invite them to suggest examples of when boys and girls are treated differently that they feel are unfair.
- Read out the passage from pages 6 and 7 when Bill arrives at school, from 'The headteacher was standing at the school gates...' up to 'We don't want to miss assembly, do we?' Ask the children how the headteacher treats Bill differently to the boys. Do they think it is fair? How do they think he could have reacted that would have been fair?
- Hand out copies of photocopiable page 15 and scissors. Tell the children to work in pairs, read the examples and decide which are fair and which are unfair. Ask them to cut out the passages and put them into two piles.
- Encourage the pairs to hold up a 'fair' example, read it out and invite the class to vote to see if they agree. Repeat with other examples.
- Compare and contrast the pairs' groupings. If some have grouped examples differently, invite them to give reasons.

Differentiation
For older/more confident learners: Ask the children to add further examples from the story to their 'fair' and 'unfair' piles.
For younger/less confident learners: Allow the children to concentrate on categorising just four of the examples.

What is Bill thinking?

Objective: To infer characters' feelings in fiction.
What you need: Copies of *Bill's New Frock*, photocopiable page 16.
Cross-curricular links: PSHE; Citizenship.

What to do
- Plan this activity for when the children have finished reading the story (and after the 'Bill in the hot seat' activity on page 19).
- Talk with the children about how authors don't always tell readers what a character is thinking or feeling, but they will give clues by describing their facial expressions, actions or how other characters react to them.
- Read the paragraph on page 66 to the children, beginning 'Though his heart was thumping...'. Discuss what has happened in the chapter up to this point. On the board draw a stick figure of Bill with a thought bubble and ask the children to suggest what Bill is thinking and feeling at this point in the story. Write some of their suggestions in the thought bubble.
- Show the group a copy of photocopiable page 16 and read out the author's descriptions of key points in the story. Provide each child with a copy of this sheet and ask them to write words and phrases in the speech bubbles to say what Bill is thinking or feeling at each point.
- As a plenary session, invite children to sit in the hot seat as Bill and describe what they are thinking and why in one of the situations from photocopiable page 16.

Differentiation
For older/more confident learners: Invite the children to find two other points in the story, draw thought bubbles and then write what Bill is thinking at each of these points.
For younger/less confident learners: Allow the children to choose three of the key points and write Bill's thought bubbles for them.

READ & RESPOND: Activities based on *Bill's New Frock*

Plot, character and setting

SECTION 4

The playground

Objective: To show imagination through the language used to create atmosphere.
What you need: Copies of *Bill's New Frock*, coloured pencils.
Cross-curricular links: Art and Design; Geography.

What to do
- Use this activity after reading Chapter 2.
- Ask the children to describe the playground setting. Encourage them to add as many details as they can, using both the illustrations and text. For example, there are boys kicking a ball, girls sitting on the nursery wall and it is chilly.
- Tell them to imagine they are looking out of the open cloakroom window. First, ask the children to describe the layout of the playground, focusing on its physical appearance. Draw out their responses by asking questions, such as: *Girls are huddled in each corner of the playground, so what shape it is? Two girls are marking a hopscotch frame, so what type of surface is it?*
- Now invite them to focus on who is in the playground and what they are doing.
- Encourage the children to close their eyes and imagine what they can hear. Ask them to not only think about the sounds of the children, but about other sounds as well, such as traffic and animal sounds. Invite them to imagine how they are feeling. Is it hot or chilly?
- Provide coloured pencils and ask them to draw and label the playground. Encourage them to write captions containing as much descriptive detail as possible.
- Compare the similarities and differences in their drawings.

Differentiation
For older/more confident learners: Ask the children to write a paragraph they could use as a setting description.
For younger/less confident learners: Draw up a list of features and descriptive words and phrases which the children can refer to when drawing.

Bill Simpson

Objective: To empathise with characters.
What you need: Copies of *Bill's New Frock*, large pieces of paper with a stick figure in the centre.
Cross-curricular links: PSHE; Citizenship.

What to do
- Invite the children to look at all the pictures of Bill in the book. Tell them to work with a partner and make a note of any words and phrases that describe Bill's appearance. Ask them to scan the text to find other evidence – for example, 'curly red hair' on page 3 and 'freckles' on page 5. Encourage the pairs to share their ideas with others in the class. Discuss their choices of words and write a list of adjectives and similes that enhance the description.
- Explain that they will be making notes for a character sketch of Bill and ask them what other detail is needed to give a full picture. Tell them to turn to pages 4 and 5 and to think about why Bill decides to avoid Mean Malcolm.
- Invite the children to flick through all the chapters and make notes of words and phrases they think could describe Bill's personality.
- Provide them with large pieces of paper with a stick figure drawn in the centre to represent Bill. Tell them to make notes around the picture to describe Bill's appearance and personality.
- Invite the children to use their notes to give an oral character sketch.

Differentiation
For older/more confident learners: Invite the children to write a paragraph to describe Bill.
For younger/less confident learners: Help the children by drawing up a list of words and phrases before they begin making notes on the paper.

Plot, character and setting

SECTION 4

What happened when…?

Objective: To make notes on and use evidence from across a text to explain events.
What you need: Copies of *Bill's New Frock*, photocopiable page 17, scissors.

What to do
- Children can do this activity after they have completed the 'Bill Simpson' activity (page 12).
- Explain that recognising and understanding cause and effect helps them to understand why characters behave in certain ways and how their actions affect the events in a story. The actions a character takes in response to an event can also help them to understand a character's personality.
- Tell the children to work with a partner. Ask the pairs to look through the book, find some of the events that occurred and think about what happened next. Each child should take it in turns to find an event in the story and ask their partner: *What happened when…?* The other child should provide an answer from memory. Then they should swap roles.
- Provide a copy of photocopiable page 17 for each child. Ask them to work individually and complete the sentences without using the book.
- Choose some of the children to read their completed sentences to the rest of the class.

Differentiation
For older/more confident learners: Ask the children to cut out each sentence, mix them up and then re-order them into the correct sequence.
For younger/less confident learners: Allow the children to refer to the book to help them finish the sentences.

Viewpoint

Objective: To understand points of view.
What you need: Copies of *Bill's New Frock* and character name cards: *Mrs Collins, Paul, Astrid, Talilah* and *Kirsty*.

What to do
- Use this activity when the children have read Chapter 6.
- Ask: *From whose point of view are the events of the races told?* Together, draw up a list of the other main characters in the chapter.
- Invite the children to retell the key events in the chapter and make notes on the board.
- Talk with the class about how the story is told from Bill's point of view but using the third person. Encourage them to tell you some of the events from Bill's point of view but using the first person – for example, 'When I woke up on Monday I was mysteriously a girl.'
- Arrange the children into groups of four or five. Allocate a character to each child by giving them a character name card. Ask the first character (for example, Mrs Collins) to describe the first key event on the board using the first person voice. Move the retelling around the group, asking the second character to describe the second event and so on. Continue until all the events have been described from different characters' points of view.
- Encourage the children to compare how the events appear differently when told by different characters.

Differentiation
For older/more confident learners: Ask the children to choose a different chapter and retell it from another character's point of view.
For younger/less confident learners: Provide the children with one short event from the story (about two pages) and help them talk about the viewpoint of one character, other than Bill.

READ & RESPOND: Activities based on Bill's New Frock

Plot, character and setting

SECTION 4

Stereotypes

Objective: To understand the underlying theme.
What you need: Copies of *Bill's New Frock*.
Cross-curricular links: PSHE; Citizenship.

What to do
- Discuss how Bill reacts to being a girl in the story. Ask them if he likes or dislikes being a girl and to give reasons for their answers. Arrange the class into pairs and tell them to scan the text for examples of assumptions made about girls and boys in the story – for example, 'girls are neater' on page 13.
- Draw two columns on the board and take feedback from the children. Make notes of assumptions about girls in one column and boys in the other. Encourage them to suggest other attributes and character traits that they think belong to the stereotypes of girls and boys and add them to the lists.
- Go through each item and talk about whether they are always true or always false. Can they think of people they know or have read or heard about who don't demonstrate these attributes?
- Ask the children to draw a stick figure in the centre of a piece of paper, to represent either a boy or a girl. Invite them to write captions around the figure to show positive characteristics and abilities that are not stereotypical and which they could use for a character.
- As a plenary, invite some of the children to describe their new characters orally and describe how the character avoids being a stereotype.

Differentiation
For older/more confident learners: Ask the children to use their notes to write a paragraph for a character sketch.
For younger/less confident learners: Ask the children to work in pairs to discuss what their character is like and collaborate to annotate their stick figure.

Changes

Objective: To compare the usefulness of techniques such as prediction and empathy in exploring the meaning of texts.
What you need: Copies of *Bill's New Frock*, photocopiable page 18.
Cross-curricular links: PSHE; Citizenship.

What to do
- Read out the part where Mr Simpson leaves for work on pages 3 and 4. Ask the children how Bill reacts to his father's words and actions. Invite them to say why Bill scowls and to suggest how Bill's father would normally speak to him.
- Tell the children to work with a partner and discuss what is different for Bill as a girl in a frock compared with his expectations about his treatment as a boy. Encourage them to flick through the book finding examples of how he is treated as a girl and his reactions.
- Invite the pairs to share their findings with the class, giving reasons for Bill's reactions and suggesting how he would have liked to have been treated.
- Provide the children with copies of photocopiable page 18. Ask them to read the sentences in the column 'Bill as a girl' and then in the adjacent column write down a sentence to say how Bill would have been treated as a boy in each situation.
- Ask the children to share their ideas of how Bill would have been treated as a boy. Discuss their answers and compare any different ideas.

Differentiation
For older/more confident learners: Invite the children to find other examples of how Bill is treated as a girl and to explain how his treatment as a boy would have differed.
For younger/less confident learners: Work with the children in small groups to discuss and collate ideas before they write their sentences.

READ & RESPOND: Activities based on *Bill's New Frock*

Plot, character and setting

SECTION 4

It isn't fair!

● Cut out these examples and separate them into 'fair' or 'unfair'.

The headteacher shouts at the boys who are late but does not shout at Bill.	The headteacher picks four boys to carry a table.
Mrs Collins scolds Bill for messy writing but praises Philip even though his page is messier.	Mrs Collins chooses Bill to read the part of Rapunzel.
All the boys join the game of football at playtime.	The boys' game of football takes up the whole playground.
The boys tell Bill to get out of the way.	Martin doesn't dare prise the ball away from Bill.

Plot, character and setting

SECTION 4

What is Bill thinking?

- Write down what Bill is thinking or feeling at each point in the story.

He was still standing staring at himself in the mirror, quite baffled, when his mother swept in.

Mrs Collins narrowed her eyes at Bill Simpson.
'You're in a very funny mood today,' she told him. 'Are you sure that you're feeling quite yourself?'

There was no fight left in Bill Simpson. Meekly, he allowed himself to be led to the middle of the room.

Then, opening them, he met a cold and hostile glare from Astrid. And one from Kirsty. And one from Talilah.

PHOTOCOPIABLE

READ & RESPOND: Activities based on *Bill's New Frock*

Plot, character and setting

What happened when…?

- What did the characters do next? Finish each sentence.

When Mrs Simpson first saw Bill on Monday morning she…
When Bill walked towards the footballers to borrow the football the boys…
When Mrs Collins suddenly let go of Bill's hand he…
When Mrs Bandaraina said Bill had a 'sweet little frock' he…
When Mrs Collins broke up the fight between Bill and Rohan she…
When Bill crossed the finishing line to win the race he…
When Mean Malcolm whistled at Bill on his way home from school Bill…

Plot, character and setting

Changes

● Read how Bill is treated as a girl and then write down how he would have been treated as a boy in the same situation.

Bill as a girl	Bill as a boy
Mr Simpson ruffles Bill's hair and tells him he looks sweet.	
Mean Malcolm whistles at Bill.	
The headteacher encourages Bill into assembly.	
Bill is told off for not being neat at writing.	
Mrs Collins is more angry with Rohan for fighting than she is with Bill.	

Talk about it

SECTION 5

Bill in the hot seat

Objective: To empathise with characters.
What you need: Copies of *Bill's New Frock*.
Cross-curricular link: Drama.

What to do
- Use this activity when the children have read chapter 1 and before completing the 'What is Bill thinking?' activity (page 11).
- Read out the opening two paragraphs on page 1. Invite the class to discuss Bill's reaction to waking up and finding he is a girl. Encourage them to think deeply about the events in this chapter and draw out their responses by asking questions, such as: *What do you think 'baffled' means and what other words have a similar meaning? How would you feel in his position? Why doesn't Bill say something to his parents?*
- Highlight the line from page 4, 'He didn't seem to have any choice.' Invite the children to suggest anything Bill could have done instead of just doing things as usual.
- Read the last paragraph on page 10, beginning, 'Oh, this was awful!' Ask: *Why does no one else notice that Bill has changed?*
- As a class compile a list of questions to ask Bill. Encourage them to think of questions that require answers other than 'yes' or 'no', by using 'how', 'why' and 'when'.
- Select children to sit in the hot seat in the role of Bill while the others pose their questions.

Differentiation
For older/more confident learners: Ask the children to think of their own questions rather than using the class list.
For younger/less confident learners: Let the children refer to the story when they are in the hot seat.

Interview

Objective: To identify different question types and evaluate their impact on the audience.
What you need: Copies of *Bill's New Frock*, photocopiable page 22.
Cross-curricular link: ICT.

What to do
- This activity could follow on from 'Bill in the hot seat' (above).
- Explain to the children that you want them to imagine that Bill has told his class about his strange Monday when he spent the day as a girl. The class are going to interview Bill for the school newspaper or magazine.
- Take a few moments to talk with the children about different question types. Explain that the purpose of good questions in an interview is to encourage the person being interviewed to expand their answers and give interesting details, rather than just answer in one word, phrase or short sentence.
- Arrange the class into pairs. Provide them with copies of photocopiable page 22 and ask both children to be the interviewer and work out questions to ask Bill.
- When they have written four questions, invite one to be the interviewer and one to take on the role of Bill. The interviewer should ask 'Bill' the questions and make notes of his answers on the sheet. They can then repeat the activity by swapping roles.
- As a plenary, invite children to take turns at being in the hot seat as Bill. Ask the others to ask 'him' some of their questions. Discuss the different types of questions and the ways in which Bill answered them.

Differentiation
For older/more confident learners: Encourage the children to write up their interview on the computer.
For younger/less confident learners: Let the children produce and answer just two or three questions.

READ & RESPOND: Activities based on *Bill's New Frock*

Talk about it

SECTION 5

Funniest moment

Objective: To offer reasons and evidence for their views, considering alternative opinions.
What you need: Copies of *Bill's New Frock*.

What to do
- Arrange the children into small groups of about three or four. Invite each child to think independently about which moment in *Bill's New Frock* is the funniest. Tell them to write down the funniest moment and a reason for their choice.
- Ask each member to share their idea of the funniest moment with their group. Then ask each of them to stand up one by one and briefly explain their funniest moment to the class. Some will have chosen the same moment, so tell the children with the same choice to form a new group.
- Invite the children in the group with the most members to each give the reasons for their choice.
- Encourage the children to arrange themselves in relation to the number of group members, from highest to lowest, to demonstrate which moment is the most popular choice in the story and which is the least popular.

Differentiation
For older/more confident learners: Invite the children to write a paragraph providing an overview of their original group's choices.
For younger/less confident learners: Allow the children to use the book to select their funniest moment and to simply write down their choice, giving their reason to the group orally.

Agree or disagree?

Objective: To offer reasons and evidence for their views, considering alternative opinions.
What you need: Cards made from photocopiable page 23.
Cross-curricular link: PSHE.

What to do
- Use this activity when the children have read the whole story.
- Cut out each statement on photocopiable page 23 and prepare enough cards to allow one card per child.
- Explain that each card has a statement written on it about boys or girls or both. Place the cards face down and invite the children, one at a time, to pick up a card, read it to the class and say whether they agree or disagree. Encourage each child to give reasons for their opinion. Now ask the rest of the class whether they agree or disagree and why. Go round the class until every child has had a turn.
- Ask the children to arrange the cards into three groups – one group that everyone agrees with, one group that everyone disagrees with and a final group where opinion is split.
- If several small groups are doing the activity at the same time, collate each group's opinions to find a class consensus.
- Hold a plenary session and invite one or two children to choose a statement they agree with strongly. Ask them to present reasons for their opinions to persuade the class of the truth of the statement. The rest of the children can then vote if they agree or disagree.

Differentiation
For older/more confident learners: Invite the children to choose one of the statements and write an argument for or against it.
For younger/less confident learners: Allow the children to choose one card between two and give them time to discuss it before saying whether they agree or disagree.

Talk about it

SECTION 5

Freeze frame

Objective: To use time, resources and group members efficiently by distributing tasks and checking progress.
What you need: Copies of *Bill's New Frock*.
Cross-curricular link: Drama.

What to do
- Explain that the children are going to create a moment when the action in the story is frozen, as if they were pausing a film. Choose a scene from the story to demonstrate – for example, when Bill crosses the finishing line in the race. Together, work out what you would see if the moment was frozen, who would be in the scene and what they would be doing.
- Organise the class into small groups consisting of different numbers of children, so there are groups of five, four, three and a pair.
- Tell the children to look through the book and choose a scene from the story that suits the number of children in their group. Ask them to allocate a character to each child in the group and collaborate to work out how the scene might look.
- Invite each group to show the class their chosen scene as a freeze frame, one by one.
- Encourage the children watching to describe what is happening at the exact moment of the freeze frame and to say what happens next.

Differentiation
For older/more confident learners: Ask the children to write a description of the scene that was chosen by their group.
For younger/less confident learners: Encourage the children to draw a picture of their group's freeze frame moment.

Feelings

Objective: To infer characters' feelings in fiction.
What you need: Copies of *Bill's New Frock*, photocopiable page 24.
Cross-curricular link: PSHE.

What to do
- Use this activity after reading the whole story.
- Discuss the range of feelings that Bill experiences. Then encourage the children to think about the feelings experienced by other characters at different points in the story. For example, how does Mrs Collins feel when she sees the rain has stopped after lunch?
- Organise the children into pairs and hand out copies of photocopiable page 22. Ask the children to list the names of the characters from the story in the centre of the page.
- Read out the three feelings already written on the sheet and then tell the children to use the small boxes to add other feelings that they think the characters in the story experience.
- Invite the children to draw connecting lines from each character to a feeling. Some characters will connect to several different feelings. Encourage them to discuss when and why the characters have these feelings.
- Tell the children to count up which character experiences the most feelings. Then ask them to find out which feeling is the one most experienced in the story. Can they suggest why?

Differentiation
For older/more confident learners: Invite the children to find alternative words to describe each of the feelings listed by using a thesaurus.
For younger/less confident learners: Ask the children to concentrate on the feelings of just four of the main characters – for example, Bill, Mrs Collins, Paul and Mean Malcolm.

READ & RESPOND: Activities based on Bill's New Frock

Talk about it

Interview

● Write four questions to ask Bill about his day as a girl. When you ask the questions, make notes of Bill's answers.

Interviewer:
Bill:
Interviewer:
Bill:
Interviewer:
Bill:
Interviewer:
Bill:

PHOTOCOPIABLE

READ & RESPOND: Activities based on Bill's New Frock

Talk about it

Agree or disagree?

- Cut out each statement to create cards.

Girls are always weaker than boys.	Boys are more selfish than girls.
Boys are usually stronger than girls.	Girls are always neat and tidy.
All boys can run faster than girls.	Boys bully girls.
Girls are more spiteful than boys.	Girls are kinder than boys.
Girls' feelings are more easily hurt.	Boys pretend to be tough.
Boys should look after girls.	Boys are naughtier than girls.

PHOTOCOPIABLE

READ & RESPOND: Activities based on Bill's New Frock

Talk about it

Feelings

● Write the characters' names in the centre. Add feelings expressed in the story to the empty boxes and then draw connecting lines from each character to match a feeling they experience in *Bill's New Frock*.

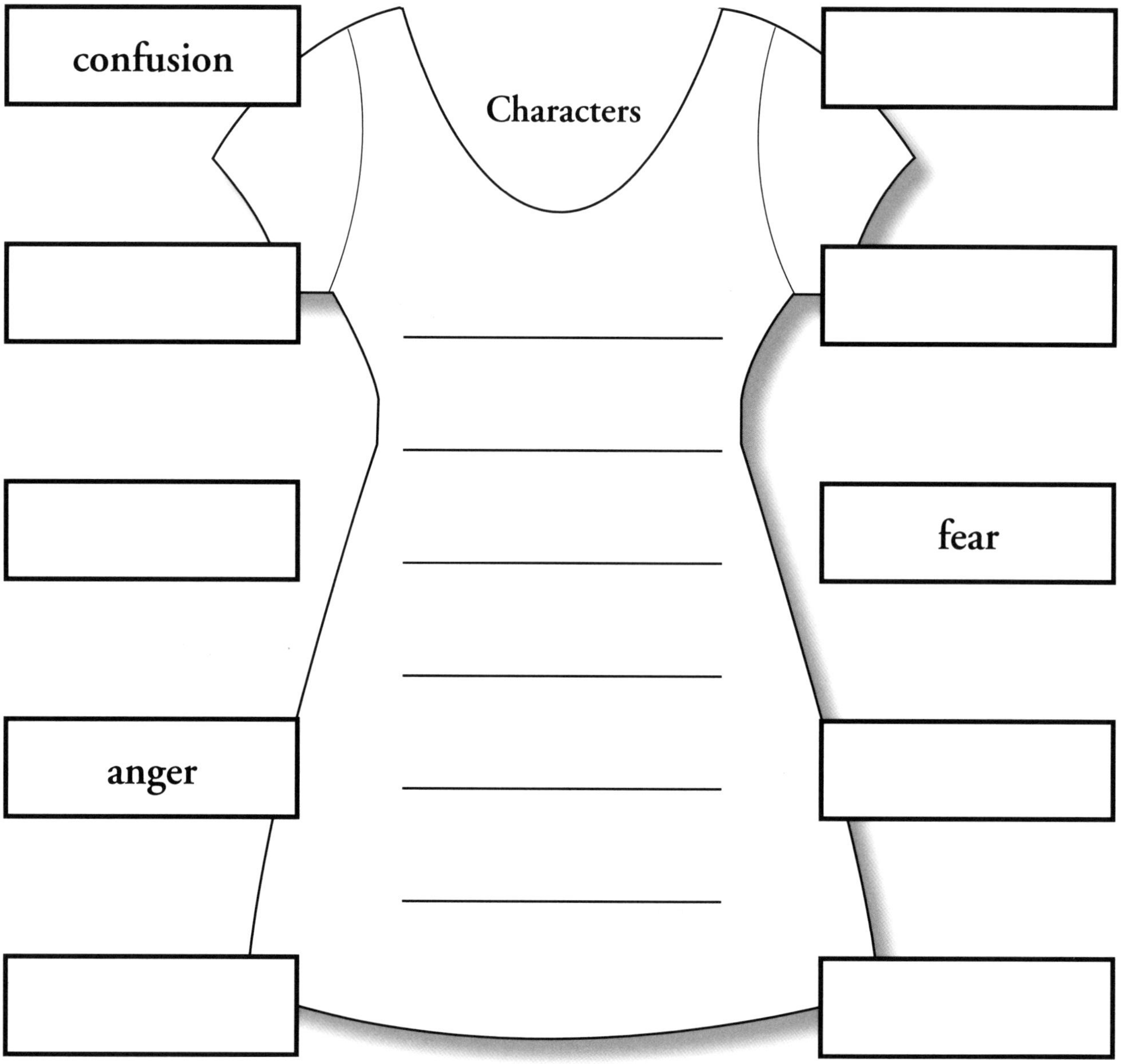

- confusion
- Characters
- fear
- anger

PHOTOCOPIABLE

READ & RESPOND: Activities based on *Bill's New Frock*

Get writing

SECTION 6

Bill's diary

Objective: To experiment with different narrative forms and styles.
What you need: Copies of *Bill's New Frock*.

What to do
- Invite the children to tell you the main events in the story and make notes on the board. Discuss the way the story is narrated – for instance, it is told in the third person from Bill's point of view.
- Write the opening sentence on the board, 'When Bill Simpson woke up on Monday morning, he found he was a girl.' Encourage the children to tell you how to change the sentence into the first person, in Bill's voice. For example, 'When I woke up on Monday morning, I found I was a girl.'
- Explain to the children that they are going to use the notes on the board to write a diary entry for Bill about what happened on Monday. Talk about the intended audience for a diary. Elicit that a diary is usually personal writing to be read only by the author and that it uses informal words and sentences.
- Encourage them to suggest how Bill might write the opening sentence as a diary entry – for example, 'This morning I woke up and I was a girl!!! Horror!'
- Invite the children to write a diary entry for Bill, focusing on his day as a girl.

Differentiation
For older/more confident learners: Encourage the children to write a short diary entry for Mean Malcolm, which focuses on the incident between him and Bill on Monday afternoon.
For younger/less confident learners: Let the children create a picture diary for Bill with a simple recount in the first person.

Class timetable

Objective: To identify and make notes of the main points of sections of text.
What you need: Copies of *Bill's New Frock*, photocopiable page 28, scissors.

What to do
- Ask the children about the period of time during which the events in *Bill's New Frock* happen. (One day – Monday.) Invite them to describe the activities that take place in Bill's class on Monday. Can they remember the sequence of lessons in the story? Remind them that the sequence of lessons in the school day is called a timetable.
- Provide each child with a copy of photocopiable page 28. Explain that the timetable is written out of sequence. Ask the children to work with a partner, cut out the sections of the table and collaborate to re-order the lessons as they occur in the story.
- Then invite them to read the summary of what happens to Bill in the first event (Assembly) and write a single sentence to summarise what happens to Bill in each event of the day.
- Encourage the children to read their summaries in a plenary session. Choose some of their sentences to write on the board. Can they make them even shorter and retain the sense?

Differentiation
For older/more confident learners: Ask the children to attempt to sequence the timetable and write their summary sentences without referring to the book.
For younger/less confident learners: Let the children refer to the book to work out the sequence for the timetable and allow them to concentrate on summarising only four of the lessons.

Get writing

SECTION 6

A new lesson

Objective: To develop and refine ideas in writing using planning.
What you need: Copies of *Bill's New Frock*, photocopiable page 29.

What to do
- Invite the children to do this activity after completing the 'Class timetable' activity (page 25). Revisit the class timetable and ask the children to recall what Bill did after the class races. Elicit that the author does not give details but simply says that 'the afternoon seemed endless' (on page 92).
- Explain to the children that they are going to invent a new event for the story that takes place in another lesson. Suggest that the new lesson could be either a music lesson or a PE lesson.
- Write a list of ideas about what might happen in a music or PE lesson that would be different for Bill as a girl rather than as a boy. For example, he might have to sing with the girls' choir, or, because he is wearing a dress, sing a solo.
- Provide the children with the story starter on photocopiable page 29 and invite them to write their own event in either a music or PE lesson.
- Ask some of the children to read their new event to the class. Have they managed to explain how Bill feels in this lesson?

Differentiation
For older/more confident learners: Ask the children to write both a music and PE event.
For younger/less confident learners: Work with the children to bullet point what happens in the new lesson before asking them to write it up in pairs.

Bill was weird today

Objective: To develop viewpoint through the use of direct and reported speech, portrayal of action and selection of detail.
What you need: Copies of *Bill's New Frock*.

What to do
- Run this activity when the children have read Chapter 6 and after completing the 'Viewpoint' activity (page 13).
- Ask the children to name the girls involved in arranging the race for Paul to win. Encourage them to suggest which one is the main instigator of the plan and to give reasons based on the text ('"Right," Kirsty said. "That's settled."' on page 79).
- Ask them to decide if Paul guesses their plan, providing evidence from the text. (He doesn't guess – this is shown by his delighted response: '"Second!" he yelled in triumph. "I came second! Second!"' on page 89.)
- Invite the children to suggest how the episode of the final race might appear different from another person's point of view. Hold a shared writing session to demonstrate how to write the episode from Kirsty's or Paul's viewpoint – for example:

  'Paul couldn't believe his luck at being in the final race, but when he saw his competition his heart sank.
  "Kirsty will win," he said to himself.
  When Mrs Collins shouted "Go" he ran and got ahead of Astrid. He didn't notice her fall…'

- Invite the children to choose either Kirsty or Paul and to write a description of the race from their point of view.

Differentiation
For older/more confident learners: Tell the children to write the same episode from the remaining character's viewpoint.
For younger/less confident learners: Let the children work in pairs and continue the story from the shared writing session.

Get writing

SECTION 6

Change the ending

Objective: To develop and refine ideas in writing using planning.
What you need: Copies of *Bill's New Frock*.

What to do
- Tell the class to re-read the last chapter of the book.
- Discuss the ending with the children and how Bill just suddenly turns back into being a boy as inexplicably as he had become a girl. Ask them if they think this is a good way to end the story and to give a reason for their opinion.
- Invite the children to suggest alternative ways to end the story. For example: Bill remains a girl for another day; Bill changes back into a boy and thinks about how things are different for girls; or Bill's mother buys him a new dress to replace the spoiled pink frock.
- Make a list of the children's suggestions and hold a class vote on which one they prefer.
- Tell the children to work with a partner and plan a new ending for the story based on the class vote. Once they have made notes for their plans as a pair, invite them to write their new endings individually.
- Hold a plenary session to share and compare their new endings.

Differentiation
For older/more confident learners: Ask the children to select and write a second alternative ending.
For younger/less confident learners: Let the children work in pairs and provide them with sentence stems to help them compose their ending. For example: *Bill was still a girl… It was another dress…* and so on.

Book review

Objective: To appraise a text, deciding on its value and quality.
What you need: Copies of *Bill's New Frock*, book reviews written by other children, photocopiable page 30.

What to do
- Provide the children with book reviews written by other children from the school about a variety of books.
- Talk about the purpose of a book review. Ask the children to suggest how a book review might influence their choice of reading.
- Hold a class discussion about their opinions of *Bill's New Frock*. Explain that their opinions are personal, so they are not right or wrong. Encourage them to support their opinions with examples from the story.
- Explain that they are going to write a book review. Using the book review examples, encourage the children to suggest what are the necessary features of a book review – for example, title, author, brief summary of the story, most/least enjoyable aspects and recommendations.
- Talk about the different sentence styles required in a book review. Explain that information about the author and plot needs impersonal language, however, when writing about their favourite part or their opinion of the book they should use personal language as this is their opinion.
- Provide the children with copies of photocopiable page 30 and invite them to write a book review of *Bill's New Frock*.

Differentiation
For older/more confident learners: Ask the children to write their book review for younger children.
For younger/less confident learners: Allow the children to concentrate on highlighting their most and least favourite parts and grading the story.

Get writing

SECTION 6

Class timetable

- Cut out each lesson, arrange them in the correct order and then summarise what happens during each event.

Monday

Story time	
Writing	
Home time	
Art	
Playtime	
Races	
Lunchtime	
Assembly	No girl, including Bill, is chosen to move the table.

PHOTOCOPIABLE

Get writing

SECTION 6

A new lesson

- Decide which lesson Bill has on Monday afternoon and continue the story.

The music lesson	The PE lesson
After the races, Mrs Collins took the class into the hall for music. Bill was daydreaming about his win in the final race when he thought he heard Mrs Collins say to him, "Now dear...	After the races were over, Mrs Collins took her class into the hall for PE. This was one of Bill's favourite lessons. He immediately ran over with the boys to get the apparatus out when he suddenly heard Mrs Collins call to him...

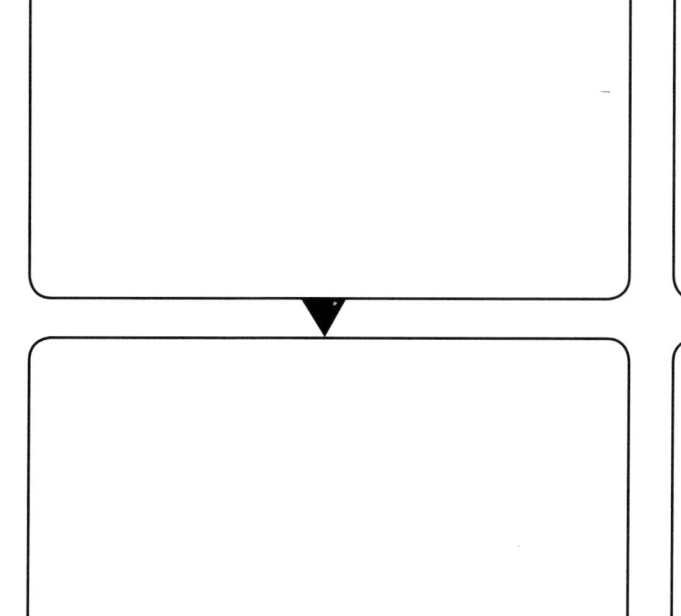

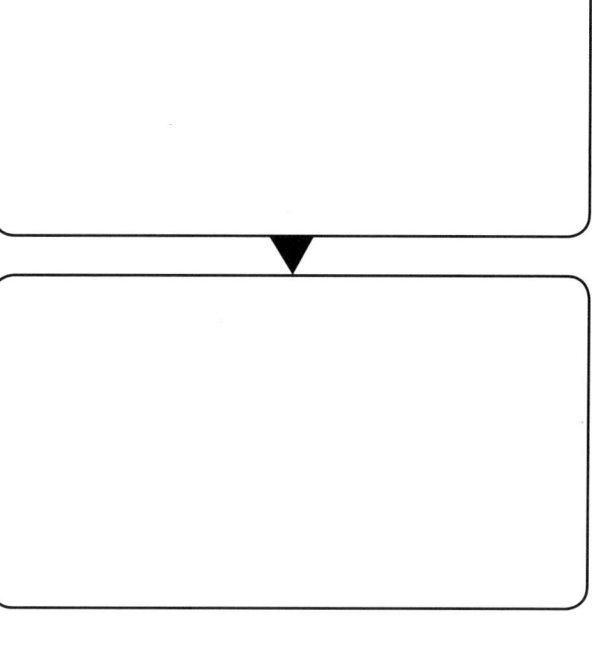

READ & RESPOND: Activities based on Bill's New Frock

Get writing

SECTION 6

Book review

Title _____

Author/illustrator _____

About the story _____
_____

The style of language _____
_____

My favourite part _____
_____

My least favourite part _____
_____

Who else would enjoy this story? _____
_____

Colour in the stars to grade the story. ☆ ☆ ☆ ☆ ☆

PHOTOCOPIABLE

Assessment

Assessment advice

Bill's New Frock is a gender-swap story written about a day spent by Bill when he mysteriously turns into a girl. Bill blames the pink frock for most of his misfortunes during the day. The author writes with a great deal of humour and vividly depicts Bill's feelings of horror and embarrassment. However, the underlying theme is about the different expectations of boys' and girls' behaviour and abilities, and how they are treated differently. This provides an ideal opportunity for assessing the children's ability to read beyond the events and between the lines to discover motives behind characters' behaviour.

Ask the children questions as they read about how characters feel at certain points. For example, when Mrs Collins 'slipped into one of her dark wet-break moods' (on page 54) why did everyone know it was not the time to cause trouble? Encourage them to support their suggestions with reasons. Ask: *Is there anything in the text that makes you think that?*

There is also a good opportunity to assess children's understanding about what is fair and unfair, what is simply assumed without evidence and how people make judgements based on stereotypes.

Humour is another of the important elements in the story. Invite the children to identify any actions, events or dialogue they think are funny and to say why. How would the story change if it was told without humour?

When the children carry out the assessment activity, their answers to the questions will demonstrate their abilities to think beyond the obvious, simple responses. The order into which they put the questions will allow an insight into their reasoning processes. The order of importance demonstrates an understanding about the importance of using deduction and inference. The order of the sequence of events demonstrates a more literal approach, as does the order of difficulty.

Tell me why

Objective: To deduce, infer and interpret information, events or ideas.
What you need: Copies of *Bill's New Frock*, photocopiable page 32, scissors.

What to do
- Provide the children with a copy of photocopiable page 32 and scissors. Ask them to work individually. Tell them to read the questions first, then cut them out and put them into the order that they think the questions should be answered. Explain that the order is entirely their choice and that there is no right or wrong order.
- Some of the children might choose to put them into an order of difficulty or of importance to the plot. Some may put them into the sequence of events in the book.
- Once they have ordered the questions, ask the children to read each one again and think of answers. Let them make notes of key points to help them give their answers. Encourage them to think of more than one answer for each question.
- Invite the children to give their answers orally, and then to choose the question where they think they have given the best answer. Ask them to copy out their chosen question and write their answer in full underneath.
- Alternatively, once a child has given their oral answers to the questions, invite the other children to assess which one answer was the best. The children can then write that answer with the question.

Assessment

SECTION 7

Tell me why

● Order the questions, answer them and then discuss your answers with a partner or your class.

Why is Bill outraged when Mrs Collins praises Philip's writing?

Why does Bill drop everything in Mrs Bandaraina's office?

Why do Kirsty, Astrid and Talilah ask Bill to let Paul win the race?

Why does Mrs Collins shake her head in quiet disbelief when it stops raining?

Why isn't Bill asked to carry the table?

Why does Bill interrupt the reading of Rapunzel?

Why does Mrs Collins punish both Bill and Rohan?

Why does Bill push Mean Malcolm over and yell at him?

PHOTOCOPIABLE

READ & RESPOND: Activities based on Bill's New Frock